GANGSTA BABY

CAMERON RAASDAL-MUNRO

Published September 2025 by Team Angelica Publishing,
an imprint of Angelica Entertainments Ltd

Team Angelica Publishing
51 Coningham Road
London W12 8BS

TEAM
ANGELICA

www.teamangelica.com

A CIP catalogue record for this book is available from
the British Library

ISBN 978-1-7397739-6-0

CREDITS:

Writer: Cameron Raasdal-Munro
Director: Rikki Beadle-Blair
Produced by: G. Riley Mills & Kate Garassino

CAST:

Cameron Raasdal-Munro ('Junior')
Josh Odor ('Senior')
Jensen Knudsen ('Pete'; 'Remy')
Bryan Nicholas Carter ('Mitch'; 'Jonno'; 'Client'; 'Rebecca')

CREW/PRODUCTION:

Casting Director: Aaron Holland
Production Stage Manager: Marz Allswede
Lighting Design: Lex Newman
Set Design: Phoebe Huggett
Costume Design: Jade Andrews
Sound Design: Zach Stinnett
Intimacy Coordinator: Christa Retka
Violence Design: R&D Choreography
Dialect Coach: Jason A. Fleece
Props: Alex Tuscanes
Social Media Coordinator: Tadhg Mitchel
Public Relations: John Olson
Director, Open Space Arts: David Zak

This extensively reworked and rewritten version of *Gangsta Baby* received its American premiere at Open Space Arts, 114 W. Wilson, Chicago, on September 19, 2025.

PRODUCTION HISTORY:

An earlier version of *Gangsta Baby*, also directed by Rikki Beadle-Blair, had a well-received 3-week run at London's Hope Theatre, January-February 2024. It was co-produced by Cameron Raasdal-Munro and G. R. Mills. The cast were: Cameron Raasdal-Munro (Junior); Nathaniel Horne (Mitch); Julian Brett (Pete); and Nicholas Clarke (Senior).

INTRODUCTION by Cameron Raasdal-Munro

As a kid growing up in Hastings, I never thought I'd be able to write a play. I was the bottom of every set, I skipped days, hid in toilets to avoid class... Let's face it, I hated school. Well, I am severely dyslexic, and only really learnt to read and write between the ages of thirteen and fifteen, which meant back then, in the Dark Ages, that school hated me. Until Miss Armstrong, at Claverham Community College, requested that, instead of the usual isolation or detention, I be sent to her Drama & English class.

She would sit me in her office, give me a play text and allow me to watch that play on Theatre Live as I followed the lines. The first play I watched was *Taming Of The Shrew* – very appropriate for the unteachable student – and as I watched Kate kick shit out Petruchio, something else hit me – boom: I had found my calling.

Drama school was a new beginning... that felt like another dead end. I'd stumble through monologues as fellow students and teachers patiently sat through a five-minute monologue that was taking half an hour to end. My childhood traumas raced forward to catch up with me, and addiction took over my life. I crashed out the school, fell into sex work, and life took me to a new low that frankly felt like the inevitable end.

But once again, theatre gave me my life back. I met Rikki [Beadle-Blair] at a Tectum Theatre workshop run by my friend Sam Butters. Rikki challenged me to start (and almost as importantly, finish) my own narrative. Over the next few years he taught me everything I know and, most importantly, taught me to love and forgive myself and others.

So, now I had a mentor. I also got sober, got out of sex work and slowly began to heal. And this play is the result. Growing up in a neglected seaside town, I never would have believed that in my mid-twenties I'd take a play to London, and I certainly never even dreamed that I'd take it to Chicago. But with the support and guidance of G. Riley Mills, Rikki and Open Space Arts, that's where I am now, writing these words.

If there's any takeaway from my story or life, it's that people's compassion, love, wisdom and patience – and after a struggle, my own – saved me. And I intend to honour this second/third/thousandth chance by living this gift to the fullest, and keep telling stories that can hopefully do the same for others. Starting with *Gangsta Baby*.

Cameron Raasdal-Munro

Special thank yous for all who gave their time, wisdom, guidance, work and love to make this production possible:

The King's Head Theatre, The Hope Theatre, Open Space Arts, Facility Theatre, Tom Ratcliffe, Tom Wright, John R Gordon, Rikki Beadle-Blair, Team Angelica, David Zak, G. Riley Mills, Sam Butters, Tectum Theatre, Claudia Phaa Rowe, Matt

Sullivan, Kate Garassino, Kirk Anderson, Phil Bartlett, Sadie Mills, Jo Mills, Sawyer Mills, Gary Beadle, Riffy Ahmed, Julian Brett, Kevin Ryan, Mark Brent, Nicholas Clarke, Nathaniel Horne, Bryan Carter, Jensen Knudsen, Josh Odor, Soho Recovery Centre, London LGBTQ+ Community Centre, Charlotte Raasdal, Jade Munro, Tristan Munro, Trevor Hayes, John Sewell, Xanthe Hayes, Hannah Hayes, Josh Hayes, Michael Window, Munroe Bergdorf, E. Harrison, Charlie O'Conner, Joel Lambert.

Dedicated to Ed Addie, loved son, brother and friend.
1998 - 2016

CAMERON RAASDAL-MUNRO

GANGSTA BABY

CHARACTERS:

JUNIOR – Queer working-class 26-year-old male sex worker from Hastings. Tattooed, defensive, torn between overt masculinity and suppressed femininity, dealing with PTSD. Seeking control of his life. Teenage Junior is a cocky, cheeky chappy, sensitivity hidden under teenage posturing, hungry for validation and love.

SENIOR – Junior's father. Closeted working-class early 40s Cockney from Southeast London. Violent narcissist, career criminal, masking guilt and shame with charm and savage ruthlessness.

MITCH – Closeted lower middle-class man from Royal Tunbridge Wells. Nervous, unsure and demanding. Married to a woman with a young daughter. Secretly visits rent boys to live out his fantasies and heal wounds from his private school experience.

PETE – Junior's stepbrother, graffiti artist, trans man, intelligent, caring, political, anti-establishment, drug dealer, loving and self-assured.

JONNO – Black, obviously gay working-class man/boy, early 20s. Joyful, feminine, gentle, flirtatious, deeply sincere.

REMY – French man, early 30s, career criminal, charming, confident, playful. Senior's ex-cellmate and lover.

REBECCA – Middle-class white woman, middle-aged, 'hipster' style, DFL ('Down From London'), gallery owner. Mature, kind, sweetly pretentious.

CLIENT – Middle-aged man from Royal Tunbridge Wells, closeted, married, dismissive, stoic.

SETTING:

Hastings, a neglected seaside town on the south coast of England; Golf Beach, Normandy, France.

STAGING:

The walls in the performance space are densely covered with graffiti slogans for the LGBTQIA+ community like 'You're worried about the wrong one percent' and the pink triangle; also with facts about gentrification and working-class moments in history.

CHAPTER ONE, SCENE ONE

It's 2023, 9 p.m. on an August night.

SFX/LX: Lights strobe, and heavy drums play.

Strobing and music stop. 26-year-old JUNIOR is in his underwear, shadow boxing, with a joint in his mouth.

JUNIOR: Alright, treacle?

JUNIOR sits next to an audience member.

> Fucking hell, you are a bit of alright. How can I be of service, my saucy handsome bastard? Of course you read through my menu and pricing.
> *(To audience.)* He didn't.
> No probs, sunshine, we can run through it together. As per my online profile, I am a twenty-three years young, tight, straight-but-curious, fresh off the farm –
> *(To audience.)* – twenty-eight years old, chain-smoking, ran through, used up, gay as fuck whore.
> Junior's the name. One hundred and eighty pounds an hour is the game, me boyo, which <u>is</u> non-negotiable. I can be anyone you need: city boy, copper, scaffolder, drill-sergeant, Viking, teacher, student, daddy-dom! You give me the circumstances and I'll be your chem-sex Meryl Streep with a rock-hard cock.
> Well, now I've handed you a veiny magic wand to wave. What's your wish? You're a piss pig ain't ya? Filthy git, love it. I'll need half an hour and two gallons down the gullet, just don't get any pee-pee on me... Result! Now we have a Dom/Sub party!

JUNIOR stands, clicks and points centre stage.

> You – pull down your cheap chinos and spread those pathetic saggy-skin curtain arse-cheeks while I roger ya

with a dildo so enormous you can see it on Google Earth. Then moan when I clamp your shrivelled balls to a car battery, stamp on your gooch a few times and make you crawl, sucking on a dummy of chopped Carolina Reapers while I pull on the battery cords like horse reins, you self-loathing, over-cooked, pitiful excuse for a cockroach.

JUNIOR crosses to a cupboard.

I'll pop a towel down in case you shit yourself like the last one.

He takes out a towel and lays it in front of an audience member.

(To other audience members:) There really needs to be a public service announcement to teach DL men how to douche. You think this job is glam? Bitch, please.

Safeword? *(To audience member.)* Pick one.

Audience member chooses a safeword.

FABULOUS. Come on then, cum slut, spread that bussy wide, put away your pride, and let's fuck like it's 2099!

SFX: Knocking at the door.

Shh! Shit, I double booked! Sorry honey, you ain't paying as much as him.

JUNIOR takes out a little stack of pound coins. He hands one each to four different audience members.

Hold this for me, babes. You'll need to give it to me later. Whenever I hold my hand out to you, hold this up for me. That's my boo. Don't fuck it up.

Second knock. JUNIOR stands.

Joint, bed, door.

4

JUNIOR takes a breath. In a posh femme British accent:

'The rain, in Spain, falls mainly on the plain.'

Another knock. JUNIOR applies body spray, one short blast, rolls his eyes, ambles over to the door, takes a deep breath, summons a smile, and opens the door.

Enter MITCH.

JUNIOR: Mitch, yeah?

MITCH: Mitchell. Mitch, yeah. Yeah, Mitch.

JUNIOR: *(Looks him up and down.)* How disappointing.

MITCH: Yeah, that's good. Um, okay, yes, alright.

MITCH sips from a flask. Starts to remove his jacket.

I'm ready, where should I put this?

JUNIOR takes Mitch's jacket.

JUNIOR: Lovely jacket.

JUNIOR drops the jacket on the floor. MITCH scrambles to pick it up and folds it.

MITCH: Thank you, handsome. You look like you've been hitting the weights.

JUNIOR: Born this way. Made of magic and rubber.

MITCH: What else were you born with?

JUNIOR: They don't call me donkey for nothing.

MITCH: Can you carry a lot?

MITCH looks down at JUNIOR's cock. MITCH sighs and smiles.

Fuck, I'm so stupid. 'Donkey'. Okay. I'm so fucking stupid.

JUNIOR: That's right, you are. Tragic landlord.

MITCH: Ah, yes! Um. Bad news, you're out of luck, posh boy.

JUNIOR: Oh dear! Can we... talk about this... sweetheart...?

MITCH twiddles his fingers.

MITCH: Fuck sake, no. I didn't come all this way for a bloody twink.

JUNIOR: Rugby guy, right? *(Posh accent)* What's the prob, old chap?

MITCH exhales shakily and rubs the front of his trousers.

MITCH: You're two weeks late on rent, boy!

JUNIOR: No!

MITCH: Yes! I'm going to have to evict you, as everyone knows that daddy cut you off.

JUNIOR: Dammit. You're right, too much coke in Clapham. I just can't stay away from the blasted parties.

MITCH drinks from his flask.

MITCH: Don't worry, there's a way you can pay. And you will <u>pay</u>!

MITCH slaps JUNIOR in the face. Beat. JUNIOR grits his teeth.

JUNIOR: What did we agree?

MITCH: I –

JUNIOR: Role play, verbal, financial and psychological domination. Of you. And that's what you're getting.

MITCH: Sorry.

JUNIOR: Accepted. What, me? Pay?! The best scrum half this school has ever seen? I'd never –

MITCH: Oh for fuck sake! No! No, no, no. You're way too tall to be a scrum half. Come on. You said you went to public school?

JUNIOR: I did.

MITCH: You told me you'd played in the school –

JUNIOR: I said I can play a player, man. Does the minutiae really matter?

MITCH: I need to see that posh boy bully in my head, okay? Otherwise...

MITCH looks down.

It just doesn't work.

JUNIOR: Alright, rugby boy, give me a position.

MITCH: He's a flanker!

JUNIOR: Apart from rhyme with wanker, remind me what a flanker does?

MITCH: He catches the wingers and big boys, he's the bully on the field. You know! The one in the showers with the big cock?

JUNIOR: Got it.

JUNIOR gently takes MITCH and positions him so they are facing each other.

Oh, my shoulder hurts like billy-o from tackling that... that...

MITCH: *(Prompting.)* Prop!

JUNIOR: ...tackling that prop. Massage me while we talk.

MITCH leaps at the opportunity.

MITCH: You're late on rent; now you want me to massage you? Oh, you arrogant, preppy bugger!

MITCH grabs JUNIOR'S nipple and twists hard.

JUNIOR: Okay, stop...

MITCH ignores him and with his other hand reaches down towards his own crotch.

JUNIOR: [*Safeword*].

JUNIOR bats the hand away.

Fuck sake, [*Safeword*]!

MITCH: What? It was just starting to work!

JUNIOR: Take a deep fucking breath, Mitch. Now!

MITCH does as he's told.

Look at me. Look at me. Sex is intimacy, yes?

MITCH: intimacy?

JUNIOR: How about we just sit for a bit, get naked together. And enjoy this evening for ourselves, as ourselves.

MITCH: But then it'd be like you're real.

JUNIOR: Sorry to break it to ya... But I'm real, Mitch. And so are you.
(*Beat.*)
This doesn't have to be so stressful.

MITCH: You find this stressful?

JUNIOR: No! Maybe, yes. It's this posh boy porn situation, it's just not... us.

MITCH: They would never fuck me. Barely considered me human. Dismissed me as a pansy all day at school. And now I have to deal with my boss's son and all his fucking bullshit, pretending he runs the place while I break my back for a pittance. I bloody well earned this. Please, I... I need to be seen. I need to be on top.

JUNIOR: But is this healthy for you? You're beautiful, Mitch. Fuck what those cunt toffs said to you, mate. Fuck this porn scenario.

MITCH: I'm not your <u>mate</u>! You're not my fucking therapist! Let me live in my fantasy! It's what I've worked and yearned for and it's what I want and need.
Fuck sake. Why can I never have what I want, even when I pay for it?

MITCH sits with his head in his hands. Beat. JUNIOR kneels next to MITCH and comforts him.

JUNIOR: Trust me, I get it. Those kids at the posh schools, they leave a mark. They used to point at cardboard boxes and tell me to 'make yourself at home'. They'd read my test results out so everyone in class could have a good laugh.

JUNIOR smiles.

MITCH: Never let you see <u>their</u> results, did they?

JUNIOR: Dunces, half of 'em.

MITCH: Dumb as cricket stumps.

JUNIOR/MITCH: Sexy bastards.

JUNIOR: They'll never get what it means to fear a final no-tice, walk round the house wrapped up in blankets in the winter, to eat meat as a luxury not a staple, and have ya mum work as hairdresser, cleaner, cook, receptionist, care assistant, to barely support her own kids.

MITCH: That wasn't my life though. My parents worked hard.

JUNIOR: My mum worked hard.

MITCH: You know what I mean. We had a nice little house, trampoline in the garden and Sunday roast every week without exception. I had a bursary but the 'rents still paid what they could. And I was sort of in, you know: quietest of the group, too quiet to even be the butt of any of the jokes, just barely there, somewhere, in the background. The non-playable character. Fuck. I've always been so close. And still I...

JUNIOR: ...was never one of them. *(Posh boy voice.)* You've always wanted your father to be like my father. Haven't you? Old chap.

JUNIOR throws a punch beside MITCH's head. MITCH flinches. Beat. Eye contact. JUNIOR starts to spar at a nervous, dodging MITCH.

You've always craved a lineage. And now you're finally financially advantaged over me, you think you can control and dictate to the object of your desire. But you know what?

MITCH: What?

JUNIOR: However hard you work and however much you earn, you will always be that middling, middle-class dayboy. Despising yourself and loathing the ones you love. Conversely, however low I have to go, whatever I have to do, I will always end up above you, with more than you'll ever possess. Less will summarise the remainder of your so-called life, old chap. And you know it. You wish you had my entitled, eternal youth; you wish you had my unearned wealth; you wish you could be me. And the nearest you can get to this golden gleaming godliness is to spend your sweat-soiled salary to have me. But you will never have me. I will have you. Again and again and again.

Beat.

Too much? [*Safeword*]?

MITCH: No! Fuck [*safe word*]! Thank you... and fuck you. I'm the fucking grey man. Sacrificing decades of my life to build your empire, working overtime weekends, birth-days and missing the birth of my every child to run your business and launder your fading reputation.
People like me, the real people, have elevated your brand sky high in society, and drip fed your ego and con-fidence just to get a sniff of your piss stains. But now it's time to demolish your stately homes, and shit on the foundations you built exploiting our enslaved, subservi-ent brainwashed brainpower. Hear us! That roar in the lobby of your Shards, Gherkins and Walkie-Talkies – it's the sound of the rise of the gloriously mediocre middle-man. The self-effacing, self-made social climber! The back-room geniuses and willing wage-slaves, sweating through our polyester shirt-collars in our badly air-condi-tioned cubicles, plotting your inevitable downfall, our obsequiousness fuelled by our patience and cunning. You, my little puppet, are only the face of Western progress. You colonized and conquered continents off our broken backs and cannon-fodder bodies. But now, sweet inbred imbecile – you are in our world. The Elites will speak the words I chose, inhale air I decide is toxic or

clean. YOU'LL ALL SUCK MY MASSIVE COCK!

This is a new age – a truly Great Britain surging forward with Saint George heading the charge of the centre-right brigade. You want funding from our banks? Favour from our social media platforms and podcasts? Desperate to maintain your hysterical historical birthright? Then crawl on your hands and knees and fucking beg, my pretty little pedigree. Next time you turn your back on me, dog, it will be to present yourself to me. And when I mount you, finally, as your face grinds in the dirt, you will see me. Oh yeah...

Quickly: I need press ups, give me press ups, if I see press ups I will get there.

JUNIOR: Fucking hell.

JUNIOR starts doing press ups.

MITCH: Keep belittling me! I love it!

JUNIOR: Yes, I'll suck your proletarian cock for my rent. But only so I know what a commoner tastes like. How does your little peen taste? Is it sweet or bitter? Come on, chav who made it out. Rags to fake riches. Cheap plastic pound shop public schoolboy!

MITCH moans.

MITCH: Yes! Yes! Now ignore me!

JUNIOR: Ignore what? You barely exist. Oh, do you wanna feel the ruling class inside you, flooding what little guts you have? You pathetic, little, wannabe, fucking fraud.

MITCH: Oh, oh! Semi!

MITCH raises both hands in the air.

Fuck you, whiskey dick! We have a semi!

MITCH spits on his hand and puts it down his trousers.

JUNIOR: I have lube.

MITCH: Fuck your lube, we're going dry raw dog, you
spoiled, lazy, waste of my bloody time!

JUNIOR: Take me, landlord. Make me earn you this asset.
Then you and your other nouveau-riche landlord buddies
can inflate the costs of your outrageous little Ponzi
scheme. And the government, and the *Guardian* and the
woke BBC can lecture me that you are the true victim
while they ignore my suffering and my endangered rich
white boy crumbling societal status as if they didn't owe
everything they have to me and my empire-building
dynasty.

MITCH: Oh, fuck yeah. I'm the desirable centrist, the sexy
swing-voter slumped outside a pub in Surrey, beer and
fag in one hand, Cocker Spaniel in the other. Recycling
while I dream of being invited onto a private jet to
Davos. Mock me! Let me know what society needs from
your lofty point of privilege!
(Beat.)
Can we start kissing?

JUNIOR moves in on MITCH, MITCH leans in for a kiss.

JUNIOR: Kissing is extra. Self-serving royalist.

MITCH: Pretentious supremacist.

JUNIOR: Deluded capitalist.

MITCH: Thieving fascist!

JUNIOR: Hypocritical liberal!

MITCH: Why is it so hot when you belittle me?

JUNIOR: You know why, you filthy fucking cheating cuck! I bet your boss fucks your wife!

MITCH looks down at his cock and beams.

JUNIOR: Well hello there, big boy.

MITCH: Hi buddy, been a while! Condom?

JUNIOR produces a condom.

SFX: Fade up sounds of the seaside.

JUNIOR: Condom.

SFX: The building's entry buzzer sounds. MITCH looks down at his cock.

MITCH: Fuck!

CHAPTER ONE, SCENE TWO

Midday, summer 2006. The beach, next to a sewage pipe.

SFX/LX: The stage floods with deep blue light. A melodic beat plays over the sounds of the ocean.

JUNIOR is centre stage. PETE enters and dresses JUNIOR in his childhood clothes. Music stops, lights turn to daylight.

PETE aged 12 and JUNIOR now 8 sit on the beach. JUNIOR holds a children's book and squirms as PETE tattoos his arm with a single needle.

JUNIOR: And... the, err... ca... ca...ti... Cati? Cati...

PETE: Break up the word.

JUNIOR: Just tell me!

PETE: Don't yell at me. Stay still. Bloody whinge bag. Stay. Still. Take a breath, look around, tell me what you see.

JUNIOR: *(Calming down.)* ...Pipe... Stones... Waves... You...
Needle... Ink... *(Reading.)* Cater...pillar. Caterpillar!

PETE: Stop moving, bruv.

JUNIOR: I ain't very good at being still, bruv.

PETE takes a joint out of his pocket.

'Zat weed?

*JUNIOR throws the book aside. PETE sparks the joint with a
lighter, passes it to JUNIOR, who tokes, coughs profusely.
They both smile and laugh.*

PETE: I think this is my best one yet.

JUNIOR lifts up his other wrist to show the tattoo there.

JUNIOR: Better than the sperm and egg?

PETE: Oh, I'll never be able to top that.
Your mum's gonna kill me, ain't she?

JUNIOR: She won't notice.

PETE: She is going through a lot, mate. I heard her crying
with my mum in their room.

JUNIOR: ...Just want Dad to come home.

PETE: Ain't exactly what fathers do down here.

JUNIOR: He's proper busy. Ain't even got time for a call...

PETE: Or a text.

JUNIOR: Wait till ya meet him, he's a proper geeza. Where's
Dubai? Mum says he's stuck working in Du–

PETE: – Wherever he is, he put himself there.

JUNIOR: What?

PETE: Nothing. All done!

JUNIOR: Fucking sick! What is it?

PETE: A tombstone.

JUNIOR: Ahhhh! Fucking siiiiiick!

JUNIOR clambers up onto the sewage pipe.

PETE: *(Warning.)* Easy! You'll get an infection, piss and shit coming out that pipe.

JUNIOR, pigeon-stepping heel to toe up and down the pipe, is blissfully unaware.

You're happy, right?

JUNIOR: Yeah, why wouldn't I be?

PETE: Nothing bro, I just wanted to make sure. You know we're different, yeah?

JUNIOR: Different how?

PETE: Bit like our mums.

JUNIOR: Do you know what you want to be when you're big?

PETE: I don't, mate. It's hard to get an apprenticeship, but I enjoy tattooing –

JUNIOR: And graffitti-ing.

PETE: Fuck all money in that.

JUNIOR: You'd be like King Robbo or summink. Proper famous.

PETE: Bollocks to that.

JUNIOR: I want to be famous –

PETE: Oh yeah?

JUNIOR: Famous people have the best lives! They are beautiful, talented and, most importantly, so rich that they ain't gotta pay for nothing –

PETE: They are insecure, followed, pestered and isolated from normal society.

JUNIOR walks to the end of the pipe and stares out at the ocean.

JUNIOR: I don't want to end up like everyone else down here, stuck. I want roses and applause, baby!

You see him, that homeless bloke down bottle alley?

PETE: The ex-military one?

JUNIOR: No, the smackhead beside him.

PETE: They're both smackheads.

JUNIOR: Well, that's gonna be me. I'm thick as pig shit. Smack is my future prospects. This town is just misery.

PETE: Using words like misery in Year 4. Yeah, you're proper thick.

JUNIOR: Pete, mate. I can't even read.

PETE: What about a world champion boxer? You're good at that...

JUNIOR: I hate hurting people.

PETE: A singer, then!

JUNIOR: Can't sing.

PETE: Christ, man. A dancer? You've got some moves.

JUNIOR: Have a day off, I have dyspraxia.

PETE: How about a writer? You've certainly had enough trauma.

JUNIOR: I can't read a fucking book for toddlers!

PETE: Yet.

JUNIOR deflates. PETE climbs up on the pipe next to him.

Why don't you just be Junior?

JUNIOR: No one loves Junior. I hate Junior.

PETE: I don't. *(Beat.)* I heard what you tried to do... the other night.

JUNIOR: That was just... I... get a bit sad sometimes... and I feel like I don't want to be here anymore.

I know it's proper stupid.

PETE: No, no bro. *(PETE takes JUNIOR's hands.)* You ever get to that place again...

JUNIOR: I won't...

PETE: Well, if you do, call me.

JUNIOR: Leave it out...

PETE: Please, believe you me, I get it.

JUNIOR: Have a day off, bruv.

PETE I will if you will... bruv.

PETE holds up his hands like a coach. JUNIOR throws punches, matching the combinations.

One, one, two.

JUNIOR: If I was famous, yeah –

PETE: Two, one, two.

JUNIOR: – I could pay for your shots and you wouldn't have to buy that dutty shit from the gym on Bohemia Road –

PETE: Three, one, one!

Enter SENIOR. Here in 2006 he is calm, clean and confident.

SENIOR: Look at you, little Ricky Hatton. Beautiful boy. Spit of your old man, eh?

JUNIOR: Dad? Dad!

JUNIOR runs and hugs his father.

Mum never told me you was home! I missed you so much.

SENIOR: I missed you double, son.

JUNIOR: How was Dubai? Did you go up the Burj Khalifa?

SENIOR breaks away from his son and looks at PETE.

SENIOR: Who's this lovely young lady? One of your girl-friends?

PETE: I'm his stepbrother, Pete. Nice to meet you.

PETE holds out his hand. SENIOR ignores it.

SENIOR: Okay, 'Pete'. Fucking hell, what is this world?

PETE: It's corrupt. Violent criminals walk the streets.

SENIOR and PETE beam death stares at each other.

Enter JONNO, a nineteen-year-old black man in flares and a cropped tee-shirt. He waves flirtatiously at SENIOR.
The others don't seem to see JONNO.

SENIOR: *(Unnerved.)* Whatever, freak.

Come on, Junior, we need to go. Need to get all your shit in the Lexus before your mum gets home from work.

JUNIOR: Lexus?

PETE: All his shit?

SENIOR: Yeah, we've missed a lot of time, eh? We've got a lot of catching up to do. I've bought a flat in St. Leonards. Junior's gonna live with this old bag of bones for while. Things are about to change, my boy. You want to come with me, right?

JUNIOR: Yeah, course.

PETE: Do our mums know about this?

SENIOR: How about you worry about your poof family and I'll worry about mine? Tell you what, love, have this...

SENIOR takes an envelope from an inside jacket pocket. He tries to hand it to PETE. PETE looks at him, grits his teeth, doesn't take it.

Junior, give this to your girlfriend.

SENIOR hands the money to JUNIOR. To PETE:

See it as pocket money, sweetheart.

PETE: Don't call me that.

SENIOR: You got a cock swinging in between there?

JUNIOR: *(To PETE.)* Sorry –

SENIOR: Don't apologise, she needs to hear it.

JUNIOR: Take it, mate. Use it for your shots.

PETE closes his eyes, takes a deep breath and snatches the envelope from JUNIOR.

SENIOR: You're welcome, if you've got any left over, I'd use some of it for hair extensions. How about an 'oliday?

JUNIOR: 'Oliday?

SENIOR grabs his son's wrist and they start walking away. PETE calls after them:

PETE: What about school? Junior! Call me if you need anything, okay?

SENIOR: He's pukka, ain'tcha, mate?

JUNIOR and SENIOR exit, leaving PETE alone onstage. He exhales, puts the money in his pocket, and slowly and aimlessly makes his way off stage.

CHAPTER ONE, SCENE THREE

2023. LX/SFX: Strobe lighting and heavy drums.

JUNIOR is now 26 again.

MITCH enters and undresses JUNIOR. Music and strobes stop. MITCH and JUNIOR return to their starting positions.

SFX: Buzz.

JUNIOR picks up his earphones and slips them onto MITCH'S head.

JUNIOR: This may take a second.

MITCH opens his mouth.

No, it won't eat into your time.

MITCH opens his mouth again.

JUNIOR: Yes, I'll be as quick as possible.

MITCH opens his mouth a third time.

JUNIOR: Yes, you can watch porn.

JUNIOR taps his phone and hands it to MITCH to watch. MITCH is instantly engrossed.

JUNIOR goes over to the window, opens it. (SFX: the sounds of a storm bellow across the stage.) He leans out, peering into the darkness. Shouts in an Irish accent:

JUNIOR: Christ, Tom, Your appointment's tomorrow! Lay off the Guinness for a bit, go home to your wife and sober up!

SFX: Bzzz!

JUNIOR puts on a red silk robe, goes over to the door and answers the intercom, still in an Irish accent.

Okay, I'm only letting you in because of this horrid storm. Stop down there in the hallway and I'll fetch you a taxi home. Please remember: <u>do not knock</u>.

JUNIOR hangs up and goes to collect the phone from MITCH, murmuring to himself:

'The rain, in Spain, falls mainly on the....'

SFX: A knock. JUNIOR shouts at the door – Irish accent.

All the wonders of the modern world, and you can't work your own fecking hearing aid! *(Muttering.)* Inconsiderate, impatient, wank stain. *(Shouting.)* Thomas Theodore O'Brian! I literally only ask that you don't knock on that fecking door, bruv!

MITCH looks round at JUNIOR. JUNIOR smiles and playfully shrugs his shouting off. MITCH uncertainly turns back around. Now there's an even heavier knock. JUNIOR squats down and peeks through the keyhole.

JUNIOR: MOVE YOUR FINGER! *(Beat.)* Why rob me, man? I ain't got shit.

SFX: *The heavy knocking becomes continuous. JUNIOR starts to panic, then grounds himself. He grabs the bat beside the door, uses it to stretch, takes a joint from his back pocket and lights up.*

MITCH glances over then turns away, clutching his pearls.

JUNIOR cracks his neck, very gently and quietly unlocks the door and places his hand on the knob.

JUNIOR: Just know –

SFX: *Knocking stops.*

– You might win this, but you'll never fucking forget about me.

JUNIOR raises the bat with one hand. Then begins reciting.

'Ten years down the line, you'll be walking hand and hand with your kid. Then, when you see your reflection, you'll see a scar circling your face. That's 'cause I ripped it off with my teeth and pissed on it right where you stood. Cunt. But right now, whoever you are, you still have a choice...'

SFX: *Knock.*

Fair enough.

JUNIOR swings the door open. Enter SENIOR, now 44 years old. He's still physically imposing and wearing a black suit, but now it's tattered and torn, buttons undone, and this SENIOR is broken and defeated, only standing on the legs of an inflated ego. Even so, JUNIOR takes two steps back and tightens his grip on the bat.

SENIOR: You really should get your own fighting talk. It's a sad indictment of your lack of imagination, my son. It just don't roll off ya tongue well.

JUNIOR starts to shake.

SENIOR: Still shaking like a shitting dog? Aw, little Junior.

MITCH turns around. Meets SENIOR's eyes, smiles and waves.

　　Alright.

MITCH turns quickly away.

　　Rude.

JUNIOR: What you doing here?

JUNIOR and SENIOR both look at the bat.

SENIOR: This how you welcome guests, is it? Surely I raised
　　ya better... *(Beat.)* Don't do it.

Keeping hold of one end of the bat, JUNIOR places the other end in SENIOR's hand.

Like a bailiff breaking the door, SENIOR jabs the handle into JUNIOR'S crotch. JUNIOR drops to his knees.

　　Aww bless. *(SENIOR leans in and pets his head.)*
　　Come on, admit it. You missed me.

CHAPTER ONE, SCENE FOUR

2009, Gold Beach, Normandy, France. SENIOR is showing JUNIOR a photo.

JUNIOR: That's you!

SENIOR: Is it?

JUNIOR: On a boat! It looks like you –

SENIOR: It's your great grandpapa's last photo. Took just
　　before he died out there. Stuck in a boat with no lid,

chock-full of thirty other poor sods about to eat German bullets. Target practice for Jerry.

JUNIOR: That's proper sad.

SENIOR: What a man needs to do, eh? They understood sacrifice back then.

JUNIOR: Why ain't we got any photos of your dad?

SENIOR: Can't take photos of vampires.
(*Beat.*) Burned them. Lovely flame.
Fuck, look at this. I almost forgot how much I love a beach. How the wind feels. Why I moved over there to Hastings.

SENIOR gives JUNIOR a fatherly squeeze, then kneels down by his son on the sand.

I'll never let anyone lock you up, son. I know I've been gone a while, but this is the happiest day of my life. I swear on all our fathers' lives. Whatever any of us done, even your rancid grandad, we done for you. You're it. Why you shaking for? You're safe, son. I'm off the drink.

JUNIOR gets up and wanders away from SENIOR. He picks up some stones and starts skimming them on the water.

ENTER REMY, a French man in a tracksuit. He enthusiastically rushes up to SENIOR.

REMY: Look at you!

He kisses SENIOR on both cheeks. Holds SENIOR's arms.

REMY: Mmm. Just as I remember.

JUNIOR approaches, shyly hiding behind SENIOR. REMY notices.

REMY: No? Is it?

SENIOR proudly nods.

REMY: The child of the meanest son of bitch I know, and the gentlest hands I've ever –

SENIOR coughs.

He's a lot more handsome than you, eh? Must be your mother's side. Last time I saw you, you were *(gestures to indicate height)* this big.

JUNIOR puts his fists up.

Big enough to take me on, huh?

JUNIOR: I'll fuck ya up, Frenchie!

JUNIOR starts shadow boxing towards REMY.

REMY: *(Holding hands up.)* Easy, tough guy! Can't lay a hand on you. I don't want to lose them.

REMY winks at SENIOR and they both laugh.

You see that house over there? Go in and a glace is waiting for a little boy to eat him.

JUNIOR: Glace?

REMY: You'll see, go enjoy. While the so-called grown ups talk boring grown up things.

JUNIOR: Cool!

SENIOR and REMY make their way round a corner of the house; JUNIOR runs inside. He grabs his ice cream and watches the two men through the window.

REMY hugs SENIOR. SENIOR can't respond.

REMY: Everything is wrapped, sealed and ready for you. *(Beat.)* It is good to see you. Smoke?

SENIOR shakes his head.

REMY: Pfft, all these years and you won't smoke with me? What did I do? Forget to call you back?

Silence.

You were the one saying it was just for the stay... Come on, it's hash, fresh, landed in Marseille from Morocco yesterday. Okay, okay, Mister No Fun.

REMY picks up a bulky duffle bag. SENIOR grabs REMY's arm, his hand slowly sliding down until they lock hands, then their fingers interlock. As they hold a stare, the watching JUNIOR almost drops his ice cream. SENIOR breaks the contact and whistles for JUNIOR, who comes running out.

SENIOR: Oi! Help us to the car there, son.

JUNIOR grabs the bag, struggles and drops it. He opens it and sees bricks of drugs clingfilmed and dipped in wax, and an assortment of firearms. He doesn't dare touch them.

REMY and SENIOR look at each other.

REMY: *(To JUNIOR.)* You can take out the little one.

JUNIOR takes a handgun from the bag.

SENIOR: Yeah yeah, that one.

JUNIOR raises the gun. SENIOR laughs like a naughty schoolboy and reaches out and lowers JUNIOR's hand – and the gun – out of view.

SENIOR: Fucking hell, don't go off your rocker, lad.

REMY: We're in the middle of nowhere, don't worry. You've seen this before, little boy?

JUNIOR: I'm not little!... No...

REMY kneels down and takes the handgun from him.

REMY: This is the safety. Always keep this on unless you
    want to use it.

SENIOR: Unless you want to blow your cock off and be like
    your mate.

REMY: Always check if it is loaded. The barrel and the clip.

SENIOR: It's sure as fuck not a toy.

REMY: But an amazing tool.

JUNIOR: Can I shoot it?

REMY and JUNIOR look at SENIOR. Beat.

SENIOR: One shot, okay?

JUNIOR and REMY jump up.

    Light the spliff, Remy.

*REMY lights the joint, which they share. They both hold
either side of JUNIOR's arms as he aims the gun. JUNIOR
senses and enjoys the closeness of the two men.*

REMY: Feet wide.

JUNIOR takes a wide step.

SENIOR: Safety off.

JUNIOR takes off the safety.

REMY: Now take your time and when you're ready –

SFX: Bang.

JUNIOR: That... was... fucking awesome!

*They all laugh and cheer. REMY and SENIOR share a glance
which is an entire conversation. JUNIOR swings the gun*

around and both SENIOR and REMY duck. SENIOR takes the gun from JUNIOR and tucks it into his waistband.

SENIOR: Alright son, we really need to go.

Turns to REMY.

It was good. To see you.

REMY: You too, my ugly pretty Englishman. And you, kid.

JUNIOR: Thanks for the glace!

REMY: Keep that smile as long as you can. One day you hop in a taxi a teenager, and you get out and you're sixty.

JUNIOR and SENIOR load up the car and get in. JUNIOR waves goodbye to REMY. They drive.

JUNIOR: I like Remy.

SENIOR: Yeah? Would you fancy having an Uncle Remy?

JUNIOR: Yes, please!

SENIOR: *(Smiling.)* In another life, son.

CHAPTER ONE, SCENE FIVE

The flat, 2023. SFX/LX: Strobe lighting and drums. MITCH, JUNIOR and SENIOR stand in position. Strobe and music end. SENIOR points at MITCH.

SENIOR: You.

MITCH takes off the headphones.

MITCH: Pardon?

SENIOR: Outside.

MITCH stands.

MITCH: Okay.

JUNIOR: Mitch, sit down.

MITCH: Okay.

MITCH sits.

JUNIOR: You fuck off, I'm working.

SENIOR: You fuck off, I'm working.

JUNIOR: Bollocks.

SENIOR: How much is this cunt paying you?

JUNIOR: None of ya business times ten.

SENIOR: Whatever it is, I'll double it.

JUNIOR: Fuck off.

SENIOR: Triple it.

JUNIOR: Ummm...

SENIOR goes to take money out of his pocket.

I've got another client in an hour. Wanna pay for that one up front? Cash machine's around the corner, you can pay for the whole week.

SENIOR rips the phone and headphones away from MITCH.

SENIOR: Right! –

MITCH: Well, hello.

SENIOR: Let's go, bumboy.

SENIOR grabs MITCH and starts dragging him to the door. MITCH beams with pleasure.

MITCH: Is this what I hope it is?

JUNIOR: *(To SENIOR.)* Are you gonna beat every man I'm shagging to a pulp?

MITCH: It is! It's a hate crime fantasy!

SENIOR: Give it a rest.

MITCH: Delicious! How did you know?

JUNIOR: You give it a rest.

MITCH: *(Whispers in SENIOR's ear)* Spread me wide and bring the pain, Daddy.

JUNIOR: After all these years you still can't stand to see me with a man.

MITCH: Abusive Daddy! We're just ticking off the list, aren't we!

SENIOR: What the fuck do you want from me?

JUNIOR: A childhood would be sick.

MITCH: Fuck me up! Please, I'm begging you!

SENIOR: That what this is? Another childish bleedin' tantrum?

JUNIOR: To actually be loved wouldn't be bad neither. And to be accepted and not hated for how I was born would be fucking amazing.

MITCH: Slap me! Choke me! Make me hobble out of here like my balls are fragile crystals!

SENIOR: Shut up.

MITCH: YesSorryThankyou...

SENIOR: You look mental. I do accept ya. I don't love it and you know I can't love it. But there's loads of queens and

muscle marys in prison, and some of them are alright. So...
Look, son, I don't really want to be having this conversation, but what I'm trying to say is, you're alright. Let's talk about this later.
(Turns to MITCH.)
You know who I'm actually here for, doncha, Mitch? You just had to buy the big house, dincha? The gazebo, the trampoline, the back garden pizza-oven and the four-wheel drive. You've buried your head in a pile of un-opened bills, racked up these debts and still couldn't bring yourself to sell your daughter's pony.

MITCH: Who are you?

SENIOR: You know who I am.

MITCH: Surely you work for...?

Points at JUNIOR.

SENIOR: You know exactly who I work for.

MITCH: You're...

SENIOR: The debt collector.

MITCH: I have to go.

SENIOR: Yeah. With me.

MITCH looks helplessly at JUNIOR.

SENIOR: Your wife and daughter have such lovely expensive teeth, it would be a shame if someone... decorated the cobbles with them...

MITCH: How'd you know I have a daughter?

JUNIOR: Lucky guess. It's all bullshit, he doesn't like that I'm fucking a bloke.

MITCH: How does he know my name?

JUNIOR: He heard me say it. This is all about me and him.

SENIOR: Pull your head out your arse.

JUNIOR: I will, if you let me do my job.

SENIOR: I will, if you let me do my job.

MITCH: This isn't role play, is it?

JUNIOR pushes SENIOR in the direction of the door.

JUNIOR: Fucking hell. You're still all problems and no solutions, ain't cha?

SENIOR: Cheeky fucker, you're living in my flat. The cash I'll get from this cunt'll be my solution, and I'm selling this shit-hole and going Italy, baby.

JUNIOR: Oh, of course. You're here for the flat. So I'm homeless as well as fatherless.

SENIOR looks over at MITCH then back at his son.

SENIOR: Fuck me, talk about a crying tongue.
(Beat.) What if I asked you to come with me?

JUNIOR: Are you high? Of course you are.

SENIOR: Oh, come on. It'll be fun. Bury the hatchet, and have an adventure!

JUNIOR: I've had enough adventures with you, thank you very much.

SENIOR: From the sounds of it you been working too much. Bet you can barely sit down. Why don't you take a well-deserved break, put some Savlon on your arsehole and have a life-long lie-down on a beach?

JUNIOR: It's actually fucking mental that you think I would go with you and put myself through that again. Why don't you do what you do best, be the world champion of abandonment and fuck off.

SENIOR: I'm not good at this, son. I need...

JUNIOR: You need...?

SENIOR: I need your...

JUNIOR: You need my...?

SENIOR: I need your help.
  (Beat.)
  There's no school for shit dads is there? No rehab.
  I need your help.

JUNIOR: You could start by accepting me for who I am. I am a poof. And I'm a slag. And this is my work and my art. Can you handle that?

SENIOR: I've seen people with their hands cut off trying to swim out of a river. I can handle it, snowflake.

JUNIOR: Prove it.

JUNIOR puts his arm around MITCH. To SENIOR:

  You want me to come with you, you have to watch.

SENIOR: You what, bruv?

JUNIOR: You heard.

MITCH: Do I get a say in this?

JUNIOR/SENIOR: No.

JUNIOR: *(To SENIOR)* You have to watch. And you better not say a single word. If you even think about speaking, deal's off.

SENIOR: Fine, deal.

SENIOR spits in his hand and holds it out to shake.

JUNIOR: Filth.
(*They shake hands.*)
This is gonna be fun.

SENIOR: Me and you have very different definitions of fun.

JUNIOR: We're ready, Mitch.

MITCH: I really think it's best I leave.

JUNIOR: No. Look at me. That's not my father. That's every thug on the football terraces that made you feel small, that made you feel weak, that told you kissing a man is wrong. That two men can't love each other.

SENIOR: Leave it out, this ain't *Brokeback Mountain*.

JUNIOR: Call him Jackie-boy! The ruffian that pushed you off your bike every day on the way home from school.

MITCH: I know him!

JUNIOR: You know him.

MITCH: He's your classic charity case, a bum living down Bottle Alley. 'Jackie-boy'... The pikey! The unwashed traveller from the caravan park on the ring road...

I'm really not sure about this.

JUNIOR: Yes you are!

SENIOR: Jesus H. Christ, can you drop your load in him already?

JUNIOR: I'm holding you. I've got you.

MITCH: He keeps staring at me –

JUNIOR: You're safe, Mitch.

SENIOR: You're men! Fuck him until he cries, screams and claws at the floor!

JUNIOR kisses MITCH's neck.

JUNIOR: I'm making love to your neck as I prepare to straddle you.

SENIOR: You're going to spunk in his eye when he worships your cock as it pulsates after your showering load.

JUNIOR: We'll climax together. We'll cuddle together. Afterwards, we'll probably cry together.

MITCH: And we'll giggle about how nervous I was.

SENIOR: Enough now.

JUNIOR: Keep going, babe.

MITCH: We'll compare bullies.

JUNIOR: And?

MITCH: Finally, we won't be alone. Finally we'll be seen.

JUNIOR: I see you.

MITCH: I see you.

JUNIOR: Do you want me?

MITCH: I want you.

JUNIOR: Then take me.

MITCH: Is kissing still extra?

JUNIOR: For you, kissing is free.

JUNIOR and MITCH kiss. SENIOR watches this, looks MITCH up and down, then throws his cigarette on the floor.

SENIOR: Enough.

SENIOR goes over, pushes JUNIOR aside. Through gritted teeth:

Stay outta my way.

JUNIOR: Senior –

SENIOR takes out his gun and smacks JUNIOR in the face, then points it at MITCH. He's shaking with rage.

FX: light change. MITCH becomes (SENIOR's triggered memory of) JONNO. Only SENIOR can see JONNO.

LX: the lighting shifts to indicate whether it is MITCH or JONNO speaking.

JONNO: Ooo, that's a big one. *(Winks)*

SENIOR: Shit, no.

JONNO: Can I hold it? I promise to be gentle.

SENIOR: Fuck off!

MITCH: Junior?

JUNIOR: Senior, how about we –

SENIOR: 'Dad'!

JUNIOR: Okay, <u>Dad</u>. How about we sit down and talk about...

SENIOR: Fuck talking! Time is cash. *(To MITCH.)* Pay your debts. Give me the fucking money.

JONNO: Is that really what you want?

MITCH: Is that what you really want?

SENIOR: Not another word out your fairy mouth, fag.

JONNO: Just say what you really want.

SENIOR: Pay up.

MITCH: I preferred the new role play, but fine. How would you like to be paid, sir?

SENIOR: Bank transfer.

MITCH: *(Taking out his phone.)* Okay, and how much?

SENIOR takes the phone out of his hands. Transfers the money and passes it back.

JUNIOR: Wait. Stop. I said stop! *(JUNIOR takes the phone and looks at the screen.)* You took everything? How is he meant to pay you guys back?
(To MITCH) He took everything...

MITCH: Not everything.

JONNO: Not even close.

MITCH turns to SENIOR.

MITCH: Your son has wonderfully soft lips.

JONNO: Like you.

JUNIOR: Mitch, please.

MITCH: He's an incredible kisser.

JONNO: Like you.

MITCH: *(To JUNIOR)* I think I love you.

JUNIOR: Oh, Mitch.

MITCH turns to SENIOR.

SENIOR: Don't say that.

MITCH: Your son is beautiful.

SENIOR: I'm warning you.

JONNO: I love you.

MITCH looks at JUNIOR.

SENIOR: You bastard.

MITCH: And I love him.

SFX/LX: Bang and blackout.

CHAPTER TWO, SCENE ONE

2010.

SFX/LX: The stage floods with an early morning sunrise. Blues music in the vein of Lowell Fulson, Jimmy Read and T-Bone Walker plays.

SENIOR, aged 30, the morning after a heavy sleepless night, smokes a spliff and sips from a crystal glass of whiskey. He downs the whiskey and opens a cupboard. Behind an assortment of tat there's a wool jumper. SENIOR takes it out, buries his face in it and breathes it in.

Enter (the memory of) JONNO.

JONNO: *(Of the music.)* Love this one!

SENIOR looks over at JONNO and becomes agitated.

They used to play this down the Swan's Arms, yeah? You were still young and handsome back then.

JONNO playfully puts his hand on SENIOR's belly.

What happened? Baker's closing down and you had to make the most of it?

JONNO winks. SENIOR bats his hand away.

JONNO: You was staring at me for about an hour. I thought, 'Here we go, another racist gay basher.' But just there...

JONNO points to the corner of SENIOR's mouth.

...that handsome little smile. So, I sat next to ya. Couldn't hold eye contact but ya could brush ya big muscley pinky 'cross the back of me hand under the table. I didn't know whether to run or cum.

Are you sure it's okay for me to sit next to ya?

YOUNG SENIOR: Free country, ain't it?

JONNO: For some of us! I'm just asking because I've heard about your old man is all.

YOUNG SENIOR: Have ya?

JONNO: Ain't everyone?

YOUNG SENIOR: What you heard?

JONNO: Enough.

...Then your eyes went all sad like a dog being put down. I can't remember how much you drank, enough to kill an 'orse, that's for sure. Then suddenly you jumped up and you danced. For an uptight little white boy you couldn't 'alf dance.

SENIOR: Not like you.

JONNO: And you made me dance with ya. In front of every-one –

SENIOR: *(Choked)* Stop.

JONNO: And you whispered in my ear...

JONNO/SENIOR: 'I ain't my father, I'm all yours.'

JONNO snatches the jumper out of SENIOR's hands.

JONNO: Still soppy and sentimental, then?

SENIOR rips the jumper from JONNO's hands and throws it back in the cupboard.

And still a drama queen.

SENIOR: Shut it.

JONNO: *(Flirtatiously.)* Make me.

SENIOR picks up the whisky bottle.

Here we go… Always had to get rat-arsed to kiss me.

SENIOR stares at JONNO as if to say, 'Fuck off.' JONNO stares back to say, 'Bitch, try me.' SENIOR takes a drink, then JONNO takes the bottle out of his hands. He examines the label.

JONNO: Oooo, fancy. Moving up in the world. I remember when we had to share a shandy –

SENIOR: I am not who you remember.

SENIOR rips the bottle from his hands.

JONNO: Rude to snatch, dear.

SENIOR grabs JONNO by his neck.

SENIOR: This is not a pub in Woolwich, southeast London. It's not the 1980s, and you are not here.

JONNO: Whatever you say, sweetheart. Dance with me.

SENIOR: Piss off, Jonno.

JONNO: Please? I don't mind that you're a bit thicker now. You know I like the whole repressed butch daddy fing.

A chink in the armour: SENIOR smiles.

JONNO: Ooo, there it is!

SENIOR lets go of JONNO and checks no one else is in the room.

> Go on, give us a proper one. Fucking hell, ya not walking the plank.

SENIOR stroppily forces another smile.

> That's it, hard man. No one's gonna call ya a poofta for smiling.

JONNO wraps his arms around SENIOR and rests his head on his chest. SENIOR smiles.

> My big hetero bloke with his hardon pressed against my thigh.

SENIOR pushes him and JONNO giggles.

> I'm joking I'm joking I'm joking. Gawd blimey, come here.

He pulls SENIOR in and they start to tenderly dance. JONNO sensually breathes on SENIOR's neck. SENIOR looks almost as if he's about to break down, but he is caught by JONNO and they glide around the space, safe in each other's arms.

Enter JUNIOR, age 12, in his school trousers and shirt. He stops and watches, school tie in his hands, two bags by his feet. We don't quite know if he can see JONNO or not.

JUNIOR begins to mimic SENIOR's dancing. SENIOR spots him, startles, his hand whipping round to the back of his waistband. But he relaxes as JONNO exits the stage.

SENIOR: Ello, mate.

SENIOR returns to dancing, alone now. Holds out his spliff. JUNIOR approaches... takes it, inhales; he's experienced.

JUNIOR: Who was he?

SENIOR: Who was who?

JUNIOR: You were dancing with.

SENIOR: I was thinking about ya mum.

JUNIOR: Oh.

SENIOR: You was premature, you know.

SENIOR starts tying JUNIOR's tie for him.

> They reckoned you'd have problems growing. Told us
> you'd struggle. Your mum was crying when they passed
> you to me for the first time. You was tiny. I looked in
> your eyes and said,
> *(Putting a hand on the back of JUNIOR's head.)*
> 'Blue. My boy has my eyes, my name, my willpower, and
> he'll have more than I ever dreamed...'

JUNIOR laughs. SENIOR finishes doing up JUNIOR's tie.

> <u>Now</u> look at you!

SENIOR inspects the uniform.

> My boy going to school with the next leaders of this
> country.

SENIOR pats JUNIOR on the head.

> I'm proud of me.

SENIOR looks at the bags.

> What was the count?

JUNIOR: Thirty grand each bag.

*SENIOR takes out a twenty pound note from one of the bags
and holds it out to JUNIOR.*

SENIOR: Don't spend it all on sweets.

Beat.

JUNIOR: Dad? Are you a gangster?

SENIOR: Gentlemen don't use that word.

JUNIOR: Last day at my old school, some kids were talking about you. What's a curb stomp?

SENIOR: Just know, everything I do, it's for you.

Still holding out the money.

All for you, son

JUNIOR takes it.

Now, stand up straight.

JUNIOR corrects his posture.

Chin up.

JUNIOR raises his chin.

Hands above your head.

SENIOR puts on over JUNIOR's uniform a long-sleeved rugby shirt from the bag. This is physically painful for JUNIOR.

SENIOR: Tasty. You're gonna be captain of the rugby team.

JUNIOR: I can't wear this. Pete'll rip the piss out of me.

SENIOR: Because she envies us, fella.

JUNIOR: Right...

SENIOR: You should really stop hanging out with it.

JUNIOR: Pete? Why?

SENIOR: People will think you're a poof. Especially them

toffs. Yeah, most of them are poofs behind the curtains when the butlers are willing. But that's their business.

JUNIOR: Pete needs me, dad. He's struggling. I don't care about toffs.

SENIOR: I say you do care. So now you do.

Beat.

Ready?

'The rains, in Spain, falls mainly on the plains.'

JUNIOR: The rain in –

SENIOR: 'Rains'.

JUNIOR: Rain<u>s</u>?

SENIOR: Rains. Again.

JUNIOR: The rains in...

SENIOR's phone rings. He answers and goes and talks on the side of the stage. JUNIOR continues to smoke and practice the sentence.

SENIOR: Alright? You found him? Cheeky fucking cunt. Right, fine, I'll drop him today. I can't right now! I'm with my kid, it's his first – I'll have it done by noon. Can't it wait? Please, mate, it's his first day?
Okay, I'll be right there.

SENIOR hangs up and goes over to JUNIOR. He takes the spliff away from him.

SENIOR: Again.

JUNIOR: The rain....

SENIOR smacks his son in the face, hard.

SENIOR: That place costs me an arm and a leg. I'm not giving you this life of luxury if you still want to act like a fucking chav. You will be up to par. It's 'the rain_s'. Again.

JUNIOR: The rain –

SENIOR smacks him again. JUNIOR starts to cry.

Why?!

SENIOR: Hard times create hardened men. Trust me. And you need to be able to take a smack. I want you to look and sound like them, but that's fucking all. Those cunts in them fancy towns and schools will never accept me, even though I make more in one month than they get in a year. They will accept you!

JUNIOR: Okay.

SENIOR: Again.

SENIOR walks behind his son.

JUNIOR: The –

SENIOR smacks his back. JUNIOR stands tall.

'The rains in Spain, falls mainly, on the plains.'

SENIOR sighs, shakes his head, and starts to unbuckle his belt.

The rains in Spain, falls mainly, on the plains! The rains in Spain, falls mainly, on the plains...

SENIOR buckles his belt back up.

SENIOR: Beautiful.

SENIOR wipes his nose. He looks his son up and down, hunting for what's wrong with the way he's standing.

SENIOR: Stand against the wall.

JUNIOR stands against the wall. SENIOR sighs and corrects his son's posture, then places a set of keys on his head.

I gotta go to work, okay? You stay here thirty mins and then get yourself to school. You see that up there?

SENIOR points to a corner of the ceiling.

That little red light.

JUNIOR: Yes, sir.

SENIOR: That's a camera. Don't let them keys drop, and when I come back you better sound like a royal or so help me God.

JUNIOR: I will.

SENIOR takes another bump. Takes out a cigarette and puts it behind his son's ear.

SENIOR: Look at that! Does suit you, eh? Watch yourself, though, mate. One day you're sorting out errands with your son. Then a knock at the door, and bam.

JUNIOR: Bam?

JUNIOR looks over at the door and starts nervously twiddling his thumbs.

SENIOR: They take everything you own and life as you know it is over. And you ain't even done nothing that day. You never know what's behind a knock at the door. Never forget that, son.

Right, practice that sentence, and get to school early. Mickey is gonna pick you up, if it's not in the Benz send him back and wait. I'd come with ya, but trust me it won't help ya. Less they see of me the better.

SENIOR picks up the two duffel bags.

JUNIOR: Yes... sir.

Exit SENIOR. JUNIOR repeats the phrase, correcting his own diction. The keys fall off his head and JUNIOR catches them. Looks to the 'camera' and says in a playful royal voice:

JUNIOR: 'The rains in Spain, falls mainly, on the plains.'

PETE, aged 16, calls from the other side of the door.

PETE: Oi, silly bollocks! Open the door!

Beat.

I seen him leave, it's okay.

Beat.

I heard you talking, mate!

PETE kneels down and peeks through the keyhole. Then as if he's talking to a baby, says:

I see you!

JUNIOR looks up at the 'camera' and covers his mouth with his hand.

JUNIOR: You can't be here!

PETE: And yet, here I am!

PETE chuckles. Then, puzzled:

What the fuck are you doing?

JUNIOR: Please, you'll get me in trouble!

PETE: Open this door right now, or I'mma tell everyone you shat yourself on the Caterpillar ride!

JUNIOR: We all shit ourselves as babies!

PETE: Last year.

JUNIOR looks up at the red light and back at the door.

JUNIOR: Fuck!

JUNIOR goes and opens the door. PETE enters laughing.

PETE: There we go, bro. Oh shit –

PETE grabs his brother's face with both hands and tilts it to look at the right side of his face.

    Junior... Your face...

Beat. JUNIOR hugs his brother.

JUNIOR: It was my fault, okay. Please, please don't say nothing –

PETE: Buddy, I can't just –

JUNIOR: <u>Please</u>. Promise me you won't say nothing.

Beat.

PETE: I promise. What time's he out till?

JUNIOR: After nine p.m. usually.

PETE: What you doing today?

JUNIOR: First day at the posh school.

PETE: Nah, fuck that. Get your paints.

JUNIOR beams, but it's short lived.

JUNIOR: The camera.

PETE: What camera?

JUNIOR points to the red light in the corner of the ceiling. PETE walks over and inspects it. He quickly sees it's a smoke alarm.

PETE: Bastard.

He pretends to fiddle with it.

Umm. Yeah, so I've corrupted the footage. When you need to do that just click that little button okay?

JUNIOR: Okay.

PETE: Let's get out of here.

CHAPTER TWO, SCENE TWO

Hastings seafront. SFX: A melodic beat plays.

The boys are finishing a mural on a wall that reads 'Gangsta Baby'. Beside it are painted a trans flag and the words 'I love my town. Even if my town don't love me'.

PETE is leading, JUNIOR assisting. Once the mural's done, PETE steps back to admire his work, then lights a joint and sits looking out across the beach. JUNIOR goes to another wall and starts to spray paint STOP GENTRIFYING OUR TOWN, using a stencil, but soon gets stuck on the spelling.

JUNIOR: How do I spell 'gentrifying'?

PETE: It's graffiti, mate. Who cares how it's spelt?

JUNIOR: I care.

PETE takes the spray can and goes to finish the word. Then he sees something under the stencil and freezes.

JUNIOR: What?

PETE starts to laugh.

Bruv, you're freaking me out!

PETE points at the image JUNIOR's tag is covering. JUNIOR

leans in and looks intently. It takes him a second and then it hits him –

JUNIOR: Oh my god. I painted over a Banksy!

PETE: Fuck yeah, you did!

JUNIOR: What do I do?

PETE sits back, very nonchalant.

PETE: Keep painting.

JUNIOR: KEEP PAINTING! Keep painting, he says.

PETE opens a beer, chuckling to himself.

Why don't I burn the Ben Eines in town and piss on the Mona Lisa while I'm at it?

PETE: Why don't you?

JUNIOR: What have I done?

PETE: Relax yourself. Graffiti is temporary, that's the whole point. And if anyone says otherwise, they're bloody traitors.

Enter REBECCA, a middle aged, middle class white woman in hipster clothing, holding a takeaway coffee cup.

REBECCA: *(Gesturing at the wall.)* Another great piece.

PETE: Where? I can't see nothin.

REBECCA: We still have a space for next month's exhibition.

JUNIOR: Oi, lady! Are youse that down-from-London lot who opened that gallery on Norman Road?

REBECCA: Me and my wife, yes. *(To PETE.)* You should come by sometime. We won't take any commission.

PETE: You fancy me or something?

REBECCA: You're a bit young for me; also the wrong gender. I'm merely a fan.

PETE stands and squares up to her.

JUNIOR: Pete.

PETE: We got a fucking problem?

REBECCA: No problem.

She turns and looks at JUNIOR's art.

Is this yours?

JUNIOR shrugs.

Very promising. *(She looks about.)* Funny, I was told there was a new Banksy here.

JUNIOR takes a wide step to hide it.

But I guess it was bad information.

She winks at JUNIOR and he smiles.

Can you keep this for your brother for me? For when he needs it.

She gives JUNIOR a business card, then walks away. As she exits:

REBECCA: I'm very persistent!

PETE: No shit, lady!

PETE and JUNIOR stare at each other. JUNIOR's face reads 'that's amazing!'; PETE's is far less interested.

PETE: Don't.

JUNIOR: Why didn't you tell me?

PETE huffs and sits back down. Starts to roll another joint.

JUNIOR: You have to!

PETE: I don't have to do shit.

JUNIOR: Brother, you can make real money doing that! You don't have to get arrested all the time, you're talented, man. What, ya gonna sell drugs the rest of your life?

PETE: What's so bad with that?

JUNIOR: Come on.

PETE: Come on and what?

PETE stands.

Be a working-class and trans inclusion quota? So they can kick me off the ladder when I ain't marketable no more?

JUNIOR: People make it out all the time. Look at my dad! He grew up on a council estate in southeast London –

PETE: – And where does he get his money? Why does your flat smell like a weed farm? What are you doing on these fucking trips? Why do you have bruises on your face?

JUNIOR: Fuck you.

PETE: I ain't stupid even if you are!

JUNIOR: Just fuck off!

PETE throws an empty can at JUNIOR. it hits JUNIOR's bruised body. He falls to one knee.

PETE: Fucking look around, cunt!
    (Beat.) Jesus! I didn't throw it that hard.

PETE rushes to JUNIOR.

I'm sorry I got worked up.

PETE tries to lift JUNIOR'S shirt. JUNIOR stops him.

JUNIOR: Don't touch me!

PETE: Bruv, I'm sorry. Just trying to see what's up with you. Are you hurt?

JUNIOR: I'm not your punchbag!

PETE: I know that. Junior, take a breath –

JUNIOR: FUCK OFF!

PETE: Junior, relax.

JUNIOR'S eyes start to water. Then he switches completely cold. Takes his things and storms off stage. As he goes:

PETE: Where you going? Come on, don't be like that, bro! Fuck.

Exit JUNIOR. PETE follows. As he exits:

Bloody unbelievable.

CHAPTER TWO, SCENE THREE

JUNIOR, aged 12, enters and stands centre stage looking up.

LX: A spotlight hits one of the audience members JUNIOR previously gave a pound coin to.

SFX of a train pulling into a station as JUNIOR approaches the audience member.

JUNIOR: Hello, mister! You look lost, mate. Just off the train? Where you coming, then?
Oh, my dad knows people who have been to prison.
Yeah, I can show you round. It's free, but remember it's rude not to tip.

JUNIOR stares at the audience member until they offer the pound coin.

JUNIOR: Oh, you don't have to do that!

JUNIOR snatches the coin and puts it in his pocket.

This way, my faceless stranger. Welcome to Hastings! So the town was popular before planes became cheap. Everyone would come down from London. Well they still do, they just don't fucking leave.

JUNIOR laughs.

Oh, I'm twelve and nine months, and... twenty-one days old. Basically twelve and ten months, which is basically thirteen.

JUNIOR holds out his hand to audience member 2, who holds out their pound coin. JUNIOR takes it.

Thanks! Oooo, this is Old Town, everyone loves Old Town. The markets filled with bits and bobs are all down there. That fish and chip shop is good; that one is shit, overpriced shit, okay, but the Old Town Fryer is the bollocks! Mum used to take us there, but I don't see her anymore now...

LX/SFX: The stage fills with colourful lights and the sounds of an arcade.

JUNIOR: These are the old arcades. Kinda like those ruins in ancient Rome but with pretty lights. Those old people are always on the slots, like zombies.

JUNIOR reaches under a chair and takes out two Cokes. He gives one to the audience member and puts the other on the back of his own neck.

Ahhhh, fresh out the fridge.

JUNIOR looks to audience member 3 to hold out a coin.

JUNIOR: No need to pay, the cashier's asleep.

JUNIOR takes the coin.

Wanna see my favourite machine? It's one of those where you drop the coin in and it bounces, ping, pong, ping, pooooong. And lands on this like tray thingy. These two big swiping arms, yeah, they push all the money along, and if you're lucky, some money falls.

SFX: The sound of a few coins falling.

If you're <u>really</u> lucky there's these stacks of coins, like, fifteen quid on them! Pete knocked them over once. He had to pick up the other side of the machine, but he did it! Maybe if I shake it...

JUNIOR starts shaking the machine. He points at audience member 4 and awkwardly takes his coin from them.

JUNIOR reacts to something touching his neck.

Oh, your beard tickles!

JUNIOR puts the coin in and his eyes beam.

We got the big stack...

SFX/LX: Sound of a large stack of coins falling. JUNIOR collects them. Arcade sounds and colourful lights stop.

JUNIOR: Fifty-fifty? That's not fair, it's your money. I can make more. Cool.

JUNIOR points up.

To the castle? That's more than two hundred steps. No, no one'll be up there. The view is mental! You're gonna love it!

JUNIOR walks the man along the stage. Stops.

JUNIOR: You don't have to be behind me, you can walk with me.
Here we are! There is St. Leonards, New town, Old town and Ore.

JUNIOR turns around.

Oh! Your umm, your, you know. Is out. *(Beat.)* Yeah, I wanna make more money. Yeah, I can hold it…

JUNIOR mimes holding a penis.

Just up and down, okay.

JUNIOR starts masturbating a penis.

You can touch me.

JUNIOR closes his eyes.

Yeah, that's fine.

JUNIOR takes off his clothes.

Ow, that hurts. No, it's fine. I'm fine.

JUNIOR grimaces in pain. Finally, it's over.

Are you okay? Did I do good? Can I?… Thanks…

JUNIOR starts putting his clothes back on.

JUNIOR: No problem mister, I'll keep it between us.
…My clothes don't feel right anymore. Is that normal?
…My boxers are all dirty, is that how it always is?
…It hurts to walk.

JUNIOR signals for another coin from audience member 5. When it's offered, he takes it.

…Thanks…

CHAPTER TWO, SCENE FOUR

SFX/LX: Strobing and drums. MITCH enters, face and hair drenched in blood, undresses JUNIOR, then sits slouched on the floor. SENIOR enters. Strobe and drums stop.

SENIOR is on the phone, holding an ID. JUNIOR is sat beside MITCH's body, scrubbing the fingernails.

SENIOR: Five eleven-ish, slim, name Mitchell Alexander Merlin Jacobs... Yeah, he's that cunt. Well, was!

SENIOR laughs.

Anyway, tell the family it's sewn up and we're all square now. Nah, sad cunt was penniless... Write it off as a tidy warning to the masses. Result!

JUNIOR: Oh.

SENIOR looks over to his son.

SENIOR: Ahh, no one, just me son. He won't say a word, standard. Like a crowbar in the Thames, he's washed of all sin...

We're getting ready to jump in the motor now. Treat myself to a bit of an 'oliday. You'll hear from me anon. Peace and love, mate.

SENIOR hangs up the phone.

All good, Batman?

JUNIOR: 'Penniless', eh?

SENIOR: Don't worry, I'll cut you in, my little seaside bumpkin. A finder's fee.

JUNIOR: A finder's fee? So, if Mitch wasn't with me, he'd be...?

SENIOR: Walking? Talking? Breathing? Possibly.

JUNIOR: Kill me.

SENIOR: We'll see. We don't usually take requests.
(Beat.)
What? I can't have a fucking laugh? Where's your sense of humour?

SENIOR picks up MITCH's limp hand and wags it at JUNIOR.

Such a drama queen. Don't like the look on his boat race? They do that sometimes. Just frozen in time. You know I had one fella, his face was stuck like a blow-up sex-doll, we were creasing up the whole time.

JUNIOR: You're fucking terrifying.

SENIOR: Yeah. It's a necessity.

JUNIOR: So what was his deal?

SENIOR: Who, big spender? Firm would of preferred him alive, but what can you do.
Trust me, we done him a good deed. He owed a fuck load more than he'd ever pay back.
On the bright side, my own worryingly considerable debt is cleared. You saved my fucking skin, lovely little thoroughbred!

SENIOR roughs up JUNIOR's hair.

JUNIOR: I can't believe this.

SENIOR: Me neither, what a touch.

JUNIOR: So what is the point in this manicure and deep clean?

SENIOR: Hey, it's a mark of respect. You're the one who decided to pretty much tongue-fuck the poor sod.

Let him evaporate, and spare him and his – fucking gorgeous – missus the humiliation.
Junior, calm down. I'm sorting it, we're good. We just need to get a wriggle on. Now, cheer up, sunshine.

JUNIOR: He didn't deserve to die.

SENIOR: If he didn't, who does?

JUNIOR: Do you know what sanity is?

SENIOR: Sanity?

JUNIOR: Sanity is living in harmony with reality.

SENIOR: Our reality is drinking thirty-year-old Springbank and Valpolicella Ripasso on a sandy Sicilian beach. We can stop off in Verona and get a vintage crate. So lock the lips for a second and turn the corners up, yeah?

JUNIOR: You know, every one of our neighbours knows I'm a whore.

SENIOR: Will you stop saying that?

JUNIOR: The police know exactly who lives here. Some are clients. And ya just fired a gun, you thick cunt.

SENIOR: And yet they ain't here. You ain't the only one with friends in high places, Junior my boy. By the time the investigation's dropped we'll be smoking our hundredth Cohiba cigars, sniffing pure Colombian off of Italian escorts' tits... Or cocks... Are you completely bent or just fuck everything? Whatever you fancy! Just hop over into the Eurozone and –

JUNIOR: – I don't have a passport, and you're an ex-con who is definitely wanted for something! I AIN'T DOING THIS!

SENIOR: I'm hurt.

Beat. JUNIOR looks skywards.

JUNIOR: God, why couldn't of Mum had fucked the milk-man?
Okay, what we doing with him?

SENIOR: Firstly, stop calling it, him.

SENIOR clicks his finger in front of MITCH's face.

See.

SENIOR slaps the dead body.

Go on, have a go, it's great for stress.

SENIOR goes to slap MITCH again. JUNIOR gets between SENIOR and MITCH'S body.

JUNIOR: Don't touch him.

SENIOR: Oi, whore. Do as you're told.

JUNIOR squares up to his father.

JUNIOR: Call me that one more time.

SENIOR: Fucking hell, thought you liked it.

JUNIOR: Call me it again and find out.

SENIOR: You really can really wreck a vibe, can't ya? So sensitive. Alright, I'm bored now. Let's get rid of it. Pretend to be useful and hold this a sec.

SENIOR passes the JUNIOR the gun.

Careful – Colts can be temperamental.

SENIOR lifts MITCH's lifeless body over his shoulder.

We're off for a stroll 'long the cliffs at Rock-a-Nore.

Exit SENIOR.

JUNIOR looks at the gun, examining the calibre, the barrel and the make. His expression of shock and fear shifts to something darker. He puts the gun in his waistband and crosses to the door. He takes one last look at the apartment and exits, closing the door behind him.

CHAPTER TWO, SCENE FIVE

2015. Autumn. Midnight. JUNIOR is centre stage.

Two parallel chairs represent PETE's car.

SFX/LX: The stage floods a deep blue. A melodic beat plays over the sounds of the ocean.

Enter PETE. He dresses JUNIOR in his school uniform. JUNIOR is now 15. PETE exits.

Enter a CLIENT wearing a cap and jumper with his hood up. He and JUNIOR get in the car. After a while JUNIOR coughs and wipes his mouth; the CLIENT does up his trousers.

JUNIOR: Alright, happy?

CLIENT: Very.

JUNIOR: What's your plans now?

CLIENT: Put the kids to sleep and pick the wife up from work. Good night's rest and back at it tomorrow.

JUNIOR: That's forty.

CLIENT: Can we do twenty?

JUNIOR nods out the car window. Enter PETE (aged 17) with a joint in his mouth. He knocks on the window. The CLIENT lowers it.

PETE: Issue?

CLIENT: No issue.

PETE looks at JUNIOR.

JUNIOR: Payment.

PETE: Why is it always payment?

PETE puts his hand inside his jacket.

> You are going to give my good *fifteen-year-old* friend here, fifty. Then you are going to give me and my girlfriend Miss Colt 45, thirty, and I'm gonna give you my dirt weed from the bottom of the bag. Then you can go back to Royal Tunbridge Wells, have a smoke and be thankful there's no holes in you.

The CLIENT does as he is told, then gets out of the car.

> Good boy, now fuck off.

The CLIENT exits. PETE gets into the car.

JUNIOR: Do you actually have a strap on you?

PETE: He thought I did, which is just as good. How's the new school? We miss you.

JUNIOR takes out cocaine and starts racking up a line on his phone.

PETE: Junior, the newest member of the bourgeoisie. Next, you'll be at Eton, then you can go to parliament and say, 'Young people today, believe they have an inalienable right to be gay.'
Oh come on, my Maggie impression always gets you laughing. Bet you're popular. Posh people love a pauper jester...
I'm doing it, by the way. The exhibition. I finished setting

up today. They gave a lot of space to be fair. Opens tomorrow. I could use someone more acquainted with toffs with me.

JUNIOR snorts. PETE gestures at his face. JUNIOR wipes his nose.

There's cum on the side of your mouth.

JUNIOR quickly wipes his mouth but it's clean. PETE laughs.

Why do you do this? We know why I still sell drugs, but why do you sneak out to do this shit with me?

JUNIOR: It's not like I can bring me a guy home, is it?

Beat.

PETE: Have you called your mum since you left?

Four years, buddy. She is this humble kind woman, and your dad's a fucking gangster, bruv.

JUNIOR: He's not a gangster, he runs a security company. I lost him once, never again.

PETE: You do know he was in prison before he took you, yeah?

JUNIOR: Stop it.

PETE: He fled to Malaga –

JUNIOR: Bruv, shut up –

PETE: – Got extradited and locked up in Broadmoor –

JUNIOR: Can't you even try to be happy for me? Where was my life going to be before he came back?

PETE: What's so good now?

JUNIOR: I dunno, maybe I like not seeing my mum cry

herself to sleep on a sofa. Maybe I like sleeping on a bed that fits me, maybe I like not collecting fag ends off the floor to salvage a fucking smoke! Maybe I actually like my life not being wasted getting high down the alley behind Poundland.

PETE: Is that how you see me?

JUNIOR looks away from PETE. PETE laughs in disbelief. JUNIOR gets a phone notification. PETE shakes his head.

Grindr? Next punter?

JUNIOR: Yeah. He's close by.

JUNIOR takes a bump and the spliff from PETE's hands.

Enter SENIOR, who kicks the side of the door. Startled, JUNIOR drops the joint between his feet. He rolls down the window to see who it is.

SENIOR: I've been looking fucking everywhere for you, dick-head! Christ!

JUNIOR: Dad, we were –

SENIOR: Oh, you understand English, do ya? Didn't know dyslexia let you do that. It's too cunting late for pathetic excuses. I don't want to hear a single word from your lazy, truanting fucking mouth.

JUNIOR: Dad, I –

SENIOR slaps his son.

SENIOR: The school called me and told me you've missed seventy percent of last term!
You've made it your life mission to let this family down, aincha, and every time I put my heart on the line for you, you give me this – *(Gives JUNIOR the middle finger.)*

I fucking fought for ya, like my grandfather fought for us. Because that's what men do, they fight for the people they love. I went to prison for you. What do you give me? That. *(Gives finger again)*
Now, you tell that insane bint what you know you need to tell her... Now, cunt! Or I'm gonna go in, and I'm gonna flatten the bitch! Honestly, I'm this fucking close to really losing it.

JUNIOR gets back into the car, crying.

PETE: You alright?

JUNIOR: Steering wheel, dashboard... Pete...

PETE: What's going on, bruv? *(Beat.)* What did he say?

PETE reaches for JUNIOR's hand.

JUNIOR: Don't touch me, you dirty fucking tranny. I'm bored of your envy, bored of you acting like you're my brother. I never want to see you again.

JUNIOR gets out of the car.

SENIOR: Good lad. Now off home, I need you to count tonight. I'll have a chat with this fucker.

JUNIOR: Dad, please, I did it –

SENIOR: Not another fucking word out of your queer fucking mouth. Home. Now.

JUNIOR exits. SENIOR gets in the car and sits next to PETE.

PETE: Oh ello, I'm a bit old for you ain't I, Grindr boy?

SENIOR: You know that old empty youth centre between here and Bexhill?

PETE: On the way to Galley Hill?

SENIOR: That's the one. Drive.

CHAPTER TWO, SCENE SIX

Abandoned youth centre. A chair is against one wall, another chair opposite, and there is a small table.

LX: Lights up on PETE with SENIOR pointing a gun at him. SENIOR is strikingly calm, almost respectful in manner.

SENIOR: Sit.

SENIOR drags one chair centre left and places a notepad on the table. He then hands PETE a razor blade. SENIOR fetches the other chair, places it centre right. He takes out a second razor blade.

I want to approach this with unequivocal fairness.

PETE takes one chair, SENIOR the other.

What do we both want?

PETE: Junior.

SENIOR: Junior to be what?

PETE: Happy?

SENIOR: Alive.

PETE: You're the only one putting him in danger.

SENIOR: Am I?

PETE: You know you are.

SENIOR: Do I?

PETE: It's the only thing you do know about yourself. Say what you like about me, but I've known who I am since day one. You think the names you call me scare me? At least you actually say the shit you're thinking. I see it in faces. I hear it in awkward pauses. I'm a big fucking question that people are too scared to ask. Cis people shitting out a hundred opinions that ain't their own. Believe me, it would be so much easier to just be a girl. But if you never know yourself, you'll never know fuck all. At least I fucking stand for something bigger than just me. And if you don't live to stand for what you love, why live at all?

SENIOR: Exactly.

SENIOR laughs, quickly brings himself back to the moment.

Who'd've Adam and Eved it? You an me, on the same page. Let's face it. we're trash – our boy is better off without us.

PETE: A suicide pact? Won't it look a bit fucking weird, you dead next to me?

SENIOR: The top of the pyramid won't ask questions. How many of you lot kill yourselves every day? Or get killed by people like me?

PETE: So you're outing yourself?

SENIOR: Better late than never.

PETE takes the notepad.

Just write to your mum, let the boy be.

SENIOR produces a bottle of whiskey, takes a big swig, then passes it to PETE.

PETE: Thanks.

PETE takes a big swig.

Goldfinch?
Me dad's favourite.

SENIOR: You can write to him too.

PETE: No point.

SENIOR: Dads, eh?

JUNIOR, 8 years old, runs across the stage and begins playing with toys.

SENIOR: Do you love him? You can tell me.

PETE watches the young JUNIOR.

PETE: Love's too small a word. He's a special one. You
    know?
    Yeah. You know.
    Only ever wanted to be loved, and this backwards,
    miserable world just shat on him.
    Never saw me growing old. But him: all I ever wanted
    was for him to make it through.

SENIOR: And he will. If we both let him.

*JONNO enters, his face covered in blood, his clothes ripped
and dirty. He stands across the stage watching SENIOR.
PETE can't see him.*

JONNO: Don't do it.

SENIOR clenches his fists. PETE drinks again.

    Don't make me not love you.

SENIOR takes out two cigarettes and hands one to PETE.

    You are not him, you are not your father.

SENIOR: Yeah I am. You know I am. Just an apple from the
    tree. Rotting in its roots.

PETE looks confused.

JONNO: No! You were beautiful with me! So was I! Before he got to us. Still beautiful as you cried and watched, as he dragged me out of your bed and slammed my head over and over against the radiator.

SENIOR: 'A faggot ace! That's what you bring in my home! That's what you like to fuck! Soil our linens, you cunt! Look at him!'

JONNO: He grabbed your head and shoved it into mine.

SENIOR/JONNO: 'Kiss your fucking fairy coon.'

JONNO: We've had enough pain. We've got enough scars. Don't do this to us.

His eyes well up. SENIOR turns to PETE.

SENIOR: Being queer don't bother me. In privacy, suck, fuck, fight, dress as a boy or girl I don't care. But love... Nah.

SENIOR looks at JONNO.

Don't you agree?

JONNO: You know I don't.

PETE holds back tears and raises his chin.

PETE: I'm ready.

JONNO: Please...

PETE: Do you mind, I can't, umm, you know.

SENIOR: Sure, kid.

SENIOR sits behind PETE, wraps his arms around PETE and with the razor cuts PETE's wrist. PETE's life starts to pour out.

PETE holds eye contact until the light in his eyes leaves. His head falls onto SENIOR's shoulder.

JONNO takes the 8-year-old JUNIOR's hand and they exit together. SENIOR sits with the razor blade.

SENIOR: It's okay. Let go...

He tries to slit his own wrist but there's a mental barrier: blade and skin repel each other like opposing magnets.

I can't even fucking kill myself. I am so cunting impossible to kill, I can't even kill me.

Jonno! Come back here and help me die!

SENIOR starts pleading with the audience members:

I am black and white. I don't believe in grey areas. It's only logical that this should be my last night breathing.

SENIOR takes out his gun and offers it about.

Shoot me. You've all been thinking it. This whole time.

SENIOR hands the gun to various audience members and gets them to point it at him.

My first night in prison, I truly thought I'd die, that my time had come. It was the best sleep I ever had. But it just never came.

I don't want to feel this anymore. Please. I have done things you can't even imagine, unspeakable things. To people who deserve it. And to people that don't. My boy...

Sinking to his knees, SENIOR puts the gun to his head.

I've asked myself, how do I keep getting away with it? It's because you let me. You watch, you listen, but not a single person here fucking cares enough to do what needs to be done. I'll keep being this way, I know I'm wired wrong. And now I actually want something that will do everyone good and you'll just sit there. Fucking silent. It's not on me. The blood is on your hands. You're the kid killers...

CHAPTER THREE, SCENE ONE

JUNIOR is centre stage, eyes closed. SFX/LX: a deep blue light; a melodic beat plays over the sounds of the ocean.

Enter PETE, with blood drenching his hair and face. He dresses JUNIOR in his old childhood clothes.

We are back in the flat. JUNIOR has banknotes laid out in organized chaos. He's been up all night trying to count them but keeps losing track. Every time he does so, he smacks himself in the head and ridicules himself. He tries to call PETE, but there's no answer.

Enter SENIOR, covered in blood, holding a tin of lighter fluid. He's been wandering the town drinking and fighting all night.

SENIOR: Oh, you're fucking kidding me. Lord you've got to be fucking kidding me! Why aren't you fucking done yet?

SENIOR spins around the room.

Where are you now, Jonno, eh? Am I so far beyond the pale and just plain evil you can't stomach my company?!

SENIOR looks at JUNIOR.

You soft cunt.

SENIOR takes off his blood-soaked shirt, throws it on the

floor and sprays it with lighter fluid.

SENIOR: Burn that.

JUNIOR goes to pick it up.

Not now! Finish one job first!

JUNIOR drops to his knees.

God, you're such a waste of my spunk. Stand up.

JUNIOR stands. SENIOR stands in front of him, his forehead pressed against JUNIOR's. JUNIOR's eyes are on the floor.

SENIOR: Think you're hard, do ya? Fight me, cunt! Shaking again, little girl? Oh, sorry, non-binary no bollocks is it? Come on, cunty or cuntess, whatever you want to call yourself, do something.
What? Oh, when it ain't a toff you're fighting or queer you're fucking. You don't want to soil your soft hands? Look at me! You think you know the meaning of hard? I'll tear you apart until you shit sideways into a little bag hanging off your stomach, and make you say thank you. You wanna live to see your sixteenth birthday?

JUNIOR looks SENIOR in the eyes.

Hit me.

SENIOR takes JUNIOR's limp hand and hits himself in the face with it.

Hit me. Fucking hit me! I don't care if you're gay, but do you have be such a fucking queer?

Beat.

Useless!

SENIOR kicks the back of JUNIOR's knees, making him

collapse. SENIOR lights a cigarette and does a bump of coke.

SENIOR: Gimme your fucking hand!

JUNIOR numbly gives SENIOR his hand.

Wanna fucking skip school, hold hands and act like a bent fucking chav, huh?

SENIOR puts out the cigarette on JUNIOR's hand.

SENIOR: Think you're all that? Better than me? You are nothing but a waste of my superior genes and precious fucking time. You are nothing without me. Remember no one will fucking believe I even squandered a second on hurting you. You can't harm what barely exists.

I hate being forced to be like this, you know? But you're such a disappointment I don't know what else to do with you.

JUNIOR: Where's Pete, Dad?

Silence. JUNIOR nods.

I want to see Pete.

SENIOR goes to exit, but before he can:

Dad, I wrote a poem. Don't worry. It's short.

'Have a good day, son,

Did you do your homework?

Have good day, son,

Can you take these knuckle dusters to school in case someone follows you home?

Have a good day, son,

Why are you such a faggot?

74

Have a good day, son,

Why is there blood in your bed?

I know what you are,

Because I've felt every inch of you,

Have a good day.'

SENIOR: You're a freak. Pack the bag then burn the shirt as I load up the car. We're getting out this fucking town.

SENIOR puts the gun on the side as JUNIOR puts the money in the bag. SENIOR reaches out for the bag. JUNIOR runs with it into the toilet (off). SENIOR chases him.

You little bastard –

JUNIOR slams the door in his face.

Come on, son. Let's not play silly bollocks. I'll get you a new PlayStation, yeah?

SFX of the toilet repeatedly flushing.

Oh, no no no no no no NO!

SENIOR starts banging on the door.

No! You fucking maniac! Ungrateful cunt!

JUNIOR exits the toilet; SENIOR goes in. JUNIOR goes and picks up the gun. He points it at the toilet door as SENIOR emerges, holding only a few soggy banknotes.

SENIOR slowly moves towards JUNIOR, testing him.

SENIOR: Come on, then. Show me you have the fucking minerals, you dozy, lazy, girly twat. Shoot me, queer cunt. Spray your old man's brains across the four walls and roof I put over your short-sighted, spoilt little head. Go on, show me how much you hate your evil old man. Because you do hate me, don't you? You're just like your fucking dyke mother, you hold that gun like a girl an' all! Dirty little poof.

JUNIOR shakes.

SENIOR: You can't be mine. Your face looks like me, but your balls ain't got a single cell of me. I should have smothered you, wrung you out like a kitchen towel and flushed you down the toilet in little pieces. What did I do to you? Give you a life? Yes, what an evil cunt I am. You never fucking loved me, did you? Say it. Say you never felt an inch of affection, just waiting like a little cancer cell for an opportunity to burn my life away.

Sure by now that JUNIOR won't squeeze the trigger, SENIOR snatches the gun from him and beats him with it, screaming 'Cunt, cunt, cunt' as he does so, only stopping when he runs out of breath.

JUNIOR, on the floor, blood pouring from his mouth, starts to laugh.

We could have been a team... Why did you have to ruin a good thing?

SENIOR, confused, angry and hurt, makes his way offstage.

<u>CHAPTER THREE, SCENE TWO</u>

Hanging from the ceiling a sign reads 'St. Leonards, Bold and New Art Gallery'. The door into the gallery is the entrance to the stage.

It's early in the morning. The gallery is closed.

LX: Spotlights come up on the artworks on the walls, one

after another: paintings and photos of JUNIOR and PETE.

The final light hits a mural of St. Leonards beach with two boys standing in the distance. Standing proudly next to it is PETE, covered in blood.

JUNIOR breaks the gallery door open. He's still bloody, his clothes are dirty and soot-stained, and he's holding a bottle of whiskey. He's heavily intoxicated and very confused.

PETE urges the audience to applaud him. JUNIOR falls into an empty chair.

PETE: Thank you! Thank you all so much for being here tonight.

JUNIOR finishes the bottle with a burp.

When I was told I needed a through line for this exhibition, of course there were a million things I thought of. My transition, upbringing, class, drug dealing, *prostitution*, the usual 'life on the other side of the tracks' things.

JUNIOR: Treacherous cunt.

PETE smiles.

PETE: Easy there, buddy. I'll be right with you.

JUNIOR: Oh, will you now.

PETE: What was the through line of <u>my</u> life? Simple. My clingy, needy, self-centred stepbrother. He's here tonight actually, as fucked and out of control as ever. Stand up, Junior. If you can manage it.

JUNIOR drags himself to his feet.

Quick round of patronising applause for my broken, fucked up little bro!

PETE gets the audience to clap. JUNIOR is increasingly agitated and angry.

JUNIOR: What is this? An orchestrated character assassination? You knew, didn't you? That I'd rock up in a fucking state and embarrass us both in front of these ten-quid-coffee-drinking toffs.

PETE: Easy, Junior. You're not at home now. Welcome to civilization, where the world doesn't revolve around your gaunt head. *(To audience.)* Let's say this isn't my bro's usual scene. *(To JUNIOR, in a condescending tone.)* Tantrum over? Am I okay to finish?

JUNIOR: Don't let me stop you. Keep twisting the fucking knife!

PETE: Sorry guys, I think <u>someone's</u> celebrated a little too hard tonight – and every night, by the look of him.

JUNIOR: Ooo I'm celebrating. Bloody overjoyed, mate!

PETE: In this collection I wanted to explore our lonely, over-romanticized lives as impotent class warriors huddling together for warmth.

JUNIOR: Fuck you.

PETE: Yeah you did, you greedy little vampire.
Here's what you've been waiting for. This collection is dedicated to you. The persistent fucking thorn in my side.
(To audience.) He'd say it's the privilege of my life. And it would have been if I'd had a life. I gave him mine, and look at you, Junior No-name, ladies and gentleman! Dishevelled, drunken wannabe chav falling apart before our very eyes. My living masterpiece!
Shall we start the bidding? Don't worry, he usually goes

cheap. Three pounds! I'll spare you and start the bidding at one. Do I hear seventy-five pence? No? How about fifty? Twenty-five? Ten? Five pennies? Oh, just take him and pass the slut around, you won't even touch the sides!

JUNIOR: Shut up.

PETE: And now for the grand finale, Junior will spare us the pain of his grating voice and hang himself in his last act of pure self-obsession.

Go on, buddy. Take your life with both hands.

JUNIOR: You're a fucking hypocrite. A jealous fucking hypocrite. But everything you half-arsed, I'm nailing. Watch me, big brother, and learn.

You! Assembled pretentious leeches and greedy, insatiable cunts! I give you the final masterpiece in performance art! This piece is called 'Fuck You, Cruel Cunting World'.

PETE: Cringe, read the room! No one cares!

JUNIOR stands on the chair.

JUNIOR: Life is almost erotically turbulent –

PETE: Christ.

JUNIOR: – a constant shit and spunk tsunami submerging the starving artist under gigantic violent waves of guilt –

PETE: Yawn.

JUNIOR: – pounding us with inherited shame-smeared fists. No lifeboats –

PETE: Derivative!

JUNIOR: – just our noses occasionally breaking the surface long enough to gasp a single breath of polluted, soot-filled air before the next wave of shit and spunk crashes over us, and under we go –

PETE: Boring!

JUNIOR: It's strangely masochistically invigorating. Fuck, it's actually liberating.

JUNIOR takes off his shirt, wraps it around a pipe on the ceiling and makes a noose.

PETE: Go on, copy and paste me yet again.

JUNIOR: This is art, not commerce. You can't gate-keep suicide.

PETE: Stop whining!

JUNIOR: Pete –

PETE: Is this seriously the best you can do? Fine. You do you, bro.
Oh, just a few questions regarding my final masterpiece: Who's gonna carry my casket? One of those people from school that barely knows me?

JUNIOR: They better be strong, they got two to carry.

PETE: PETE: They're going to say both our eulogies too? Well, for me they can just play 'If I Was A Boy' by Beyoncé and have done with it. What about you? 'Toxic'? 'Creep'? 'Supermassive Black Hole'?

PETE chuckles.

Who's gonna put their arm around who? As they watch both our coffins lowered into the mud. We can watch them at the wake, white as ghosts, and while whispering shit in their ears to drive them over the edge. Then we can all be one happily depressed, worm-riddled family.

JUNIOR closes his eyes.

PETE: Fine, give up then.

JUNIOR: Just let me die.

PETE: I'm trying but you're really making a meal out of this.

JUNIOR's an inch away from him.

Fucking hell, you trying to snap your neck or win a BAFTA? Swing boy, swing!

JUNIOR: Stop fucking with my head! You made me this way, man. You bastard.

PETE: Art is suffering, mate.

JUNIOR shamefacedly takes his head out the noose.

PETE: Come down.

JUNIOR steps down from the chair.

PETE: Stop the weeping wank, pull your finger out your arse and actually commit for once, and bloody live!

PETE hugs him, and JUNIOR collapses into him.

That's it. Gonna give me a proper fucking hug.

JUNIOR squeezes tight.

PETE: You'll be fine, bro.

JUNIOR: Your paintings are really good.

PETE: I know.

PETE slips out of JUNIOR's arms and exits.

CHAPTER THREE, SCENE THREE

LX/SFX: Blue light floods the stage. A heavy splash.

SENIOR and JUNIOR stand on the edge of a cliff, looking down at the sea.

SENIOR: Sink, you fucker...
   (Relieved.) For a minute there I thought he was a floater. *(Looks around at the view.)* God, it is stunning up here, ain't it?

 JUNIOR: Uhm.

SFX: a text message. SENIOR looks at his phone.

SENIOR: All clear back at the flat. You only need to tell the pigs that he was chatting all kinds of depressing shit and left early. That's if you're not coming with me to Italy.

JUNIOR is still and numb.

   Could you ever forgive me?

Beat.

   Can't be all fucked, can it?

Beat.

   Fine.

SENIOR dangles his foot over the edge.

   Worse places for a geezer to go.

He keeps looking over to JUNIOR.

SENIOR: Ain't you gonna stop me?

   I know you hate me, son, but say something. I get it. You don't care about me anymore.

JUNIOR: All I do is care.

SENIOR: Then stop ignoring me.

JUNIOR: Okay.

JUNIOR turns and puts the gun to SENIOR's temple.

SENIOR: Do you even know what to do with that?

SENIOR places his foot back on the edge.

SENIOR: This is about Pete, ain't it? Is it weird that I miss him sometimes?

JUNIOR: I don't hate you, you know.

SENIOR: Really? That's good. That's really good, you can come with me –

JUNIOR: I'm just tired. Tired of your banter, tired of your selfishness. Tired that no matter what I try or take or do to shake you off, you're always squatting in the attic of my brain, haunting me. Even though I've never even met you. Just what you've become.

They watch a flock of seagulls pass. JUNIOR smiles while his other fist balls.

So yeah, do us both a favour. Fucking jump.

JUNIOR presses the muzzle against SENIOR's forehead.

Please jump.

JONNO enters.

JONNO: Hey, baby.

SENIOR: With you in just a minute, babe. I'm ready.

JONNO: Me too.

SENIOR and JONNO smile at each other. JONNO gestures to SENIOR that he should talk with his son.

SENIOR: I want to, son. I do, but I need you to help me.

SENIOR looks at his son. Tears break. He smiles and shakes his head. Very gently he takes the gun from JUNIOR, and wipes his son's prints off.

Needs to look like I done it. But you gotta pull the trigger.

SENIOR wraps JUNIOR's hand around his own. Then lifts the gun to his own temple.

SENIOR: Thank you.

JUNIOR: Bruv… Dad, I love you so fucking much.

SENIOR: Because you're a mug. But I love you too, son.

JUNIOR: One last time?

SENIOR: Only if you say it right.

They both laugh.

SENIOR and JUNIOR: 'The rains'

JUNIOR pulls back the hammer. SENIOR flinches.

in Spain, falls –

SFX/LX: Gunshot. Blackout.

END